LEGENDS OF UR

I0164682

LEGENDS OF UR

by *POWilson*

The Arts Forum, NYC

NYC

The Arts Forum, NYC
Brooklyn, New York
www.theartsforum.com

The following poems, by the author, are also in his book, "On the
Side of a Fish": even if, that a king might smile, join we now, the
legends of my youth, here living on, the rising never came, come
to me clearly, I'm no better, emptied, water and sun, hearing
voices, hands and near ruin - near perfect.

Contents

- here living on

certain knowledge is what we want from religion,
and the baby wants milk that comes at a glance

my legs walk steadily now,
to a place where all of this is history
and mostly myth

the tale of two brothers,
the good one and the bad,
Cain and Abel, Jesus and the Devil,
Israel and Judea, Christian and Jew,
believers and atheist,
perfect divinity and absolute evil,
always a right brother and a wrong,
completely off or on, up or down,
never both or neither,
day or night,
no dusk, no dawn, no question,
heaven above, hell below,
ever high, ever low,
God's novel played out in physical form,
the end already known

stand in the middle strong
here living on, here living on

- that a king might smile

all of this clamor and worry,
hopeful generations dashed,
tragedy multiplied how many times,
how many billion trillion, what is the final math,
the last unquestioned, best possible myth...

so much has hung on these words,
that float out to where the faithful drift
and I can't help but wonder if all of this
is so that a king might smile?

the heart built cathedrals,
stained glass and beautiful damp stone,
ceilings soaring upward like a ship's hull going down...
the priest's small congregations waiting for a new world
left, with only these words, reaching

so speak clearly now or not be heard,
the winds that blew in claims of certainty
bring with them a deadly kiss,
while children walk hungry on dusty fields,
taught not to question,
would surely wonder now, is all of this...
so that a king might smile?

- the legends of my youth

who would have believed
the world turned ash, by a spark

the heavens emptied, recast
by the stories of a child

existence begun by a word,
an empire leveled with a gesture,
planets moved by human emotion,
an eclipse held by a stare

these are the legends of my youth
and a young man flanked by Archangels
flying in from over the clouds
to save the world
in a blaze of glory, yet to come

but that we carry these stories now
riding in cars and trains,
flying over the oceans,
while thinking somehow smaller
all of the nations and people
before and since,
somehow less telling and important

that this pack of sheep herders
and nomadic warriors
holding these few quaint tales
as if they described eternity…
held sway so long

what volcano spewed forth this gas
that has put us so long asleep?

- *it is enough*

maybe the Hebrew tradition was right
in at least this one thing
when they said *the unknown*
should not be named,

or called by name,

I can feel something falling
when I claim too much,

like a butterfly claiming to possess the wind,
the trees want the storm to come closer,
the white caps on the water
call out to the land,

what is it inside of me
that seems to want the winter
to come sooner than it will?

yesterday I saw a small red fox
coming out of the woods
with no interest in this well-lit house
and the centuries of progress
we believe we have on him

I've been so impressed by what I can question
but do not know,
yet if I knew, wouldn't there still be questions?
my ignorance doesn't prove anything

my beating heart is enough to show
my independence, losing my breath shows
my limitations

my heart beats and I will breathe awhile
and from then it isn't known

there is plenty to be, now, here,
plenty to question
my day of chanting will begin with this:
once there were Hebrew
now it is us,
this is enough

- *emptied*

religion's gone,
on a park bench, miles long
alone, waiting

once pious,
tripped and fallen,
jumped and fell

a person says there is no God
and something opens,
things spill out,
awkward, down,
edge of a shadow,
what comes next?
black brooding,
under his breath,
over and over again

there is no proving
something was once there,
no proving now something is not,
only the man in black
felt complete, and now, less

- join we now

join we now to sing this song,
the hero boy down through the ages,
under a tree, atop a mountain,
boy god over evil, transcendent dreamer,
the revelatory sage, and his father the king
incommunicado,
always being born in the body of the prince,
ever confident

- *even if*

even if the search for truth is not the highest call,
there is only honesty to lead us through
the uncertain

even if everything we thought we knew is wrong,
it is not so wrong as to conceal its beauty

even if the questions fly and turn like gnats
and we wonder, to what shall we give our cleverness

even if, with all of this
all moves towards the center and yet,
there is no point to call the center,
all is well... even if

- *hearing voices*

we sculpt a face
to the contour of the space
left at the edge of our own understanding

driving the chisel in, to make the forehead
the nose, the eyes, the cheeks, the ears,
the lips, the chin
to where the one ends, and the other begins

the good voice says speak and the other says
shhhh, don't say a word,
we only pretend to know
what is behind
the voices

Saul walked into the desert one night
and decided to join the opposition

the voice of a parent echoes in a child's head
for many years after
the parent has gone

- *tongues afire*

tongues afire
in the Pentecost
blazing in the third world
intimate grandeur
spiritual materialism
Brazil and beyond
failed primitivism's pragmatic spin
pray you well now
pray you well, now

up, up, up into the great ever-last
in the fingers of the walk-a-day
power of the vast
healed plus money
miraculous vamp
riffed religious tones
free association merged
hearts on the verge
forevermore
the emotional clergy
rocking out these words
you should be afraid
you are going to a very, very bad place
unless

- a spirit moving

on the crust of the earth
where the imagined spirit
gets up and walks around,
with the head balanced
well above two legs,
eyes seeking the far landscape,
panning the near uneven ground
where a slender heel might land
and swivel 'round

in the village,
dancers play drums and sing
steeped emotion,
salty and damp tones
sweating down a bronze face,
sprayed out in a mist

what comes to enchant the clay?
the waking mind ask,
what moves here now in all of us?

we suppose an unseen spirit
by what is moved,
like gravity
for when it goes, the ground falls back,
cool and still,
thick and dark, and silent

- one day soon

I close my eyes and see the morning sun,
and for a moment all is corrected

charged simply not to pass on the crime, the error
that is given from one generation
to the next

there is always this sense,
one day soon our quest will change,
like a boat pulling away from shore,
like a white glove falling into embarrassment

everywhere I see faces shouting into mirrors
pain, wrapped in a judge's robe

when I was very small
I remember carrying bricks
and my hands could barely hold them,
I thought the morning would last forever
and surely, the sky would soon
turn my favorite color

- *sing ambled*

rhythm speaks
to passion and boredom,
the heart and marking time,
mind's numb escape from
a finger tapping on glass
against the chin,
hot air fogged, clear again
a chain swung against stone
in the October wind
shattering glass end on end

many small pebbles on many small stones
to the edge of dim and past,

is it any wonder the spirit rose
and ran, and said

sing ambled noise in the restless wind,
like a bird chasing freedom
from the rhythm and the stones,
the marching drum
and the metronome,
the ritual words
no longer felt
still sounding

- *I'm no better*

there was a moment by a tree
and others, strangely open
an addiction to falling, wanting to fly,
expanding thoughts, muddled

the voice not heard by others
tonight again,
looking out across the water

is there someone who thinks and plans for you,
someone who can't be seen,
something that is bigger than everything?

we lunge into the present,
away from every cause that wants to pull us in,
encased by self, saturated by self...

many believe
Jewish is better, Christian is better
Islam is better, Buddha is better

all are many
in one bigger self,

I'm no better

- what should I call you now

the weather does not know my bewilderment,

the clouds move on their own,

my blood alone
in its own track
cannot detect the memories lost,
the wordless gestures,
warm breath felt so strong,
moments that seemed worth their time,
past

is this good fortune
I did not leap
for all which would soon disappear?
the rationale after chance
words, in their own dance,
in winter's frost
though even now
still my heart calls your name
wondering

what should I call you now

- unseen harp

the word God is not enough
to say it as it is,
we are held here
mysteriously
animated,
the humming heart
rung by some
invisible harp

a fragile barely seen clown
dancing, held by a just so wind,
a clown among so many clowns,
prefaced and followed by clowns,

my every breath is a question
and yet, none of this
is answered
by belief

- *one day, then*

the air is summer moist
for just a moment before the sun,
the future won, by the brave,
the shining moment flashing
too quick to catch,
the brief fanfare to the day begun,
searching for a day to end all lesser ones

a time to mark the glory of war,
the birth of a religion,
a country and these
leave no time to consider things,
symbols brought in quick,
a star, a cross, colors,
maybe red and yellow,
maybe gold and black,
and a mantra:
believers do not ask

then later when many lives have passed
maybe, there will be a time to reflect

- *addiction*

addiction
throws reason to the ground,

the heart is best
when it does not love everything,

this morning
I stood looking over a dry grass field
and repeated again and again

my body is a statue in a canyon,
my mind is the wind calling to the wind

it isn't enough for you, she said
what you prefer,
you want to tell the world as well

and that is what I mean when I call you man;
the one who wants to tell the world

- *layers of cloud*

I once thought something had willed
that I say one thing wrong to every two things right

I want to know the numbers…
how many people have lived
how many will

look how the drama comes and fades,
only seemingly unchanged

look how the sunlight moves
over the top of the trees where

my long sleep is only interrupted for moments,
by flashes of sunlight, through layers of cloud

- near ruin, near perfect

many gentle people say they love the truth
though the truth is full of many horrible things,
and some might say gentleness is just a veil
over wanton eyes

the sweetest child wants to rule the world
by way of sweetness

some would say, not I
but people go until they are broken,
near ruin,
and then they cry Jesus in the West,
Allah in the Middle East
or, please dear God wherever else

I was once no different,
when the kids were young
every day I said dear God
please keep my children safe,
I knew nothing and still I prayed
to be known,
I saw nothing and still I prayed
I was not alone

but now
the trees wave their shadows across my face
and my cheeks go from warm to cool,
the birds sing in the damp wood across the way
and I close my eyes
and hope for tears

if there were only tears,
this moment would be near perfect

- *even if*

even if the search for truth
is not the highest call,
there is only honesty to lead us to
the beautiful uncertain

even if everything we thought we knew
is wrong,
it is not so wrong as to conceal
it's beauty

even if the questions fly
and turn like gnats in light
and we wonder
to what shall we give our cleverness
and why does the sky turn dark
with the slightest turn

even if
with all of this
all moves towards the center and yet
there is no point
to call the center,
all is well

even if

- *water and sun*

I once called to the nameless
with many different names
and no voice answered,
the only voice I could hear,
I know as mine
or others, remembered,
the only answer
a feeling of calm,
or not calm

a plant asks to grow,
the answer is water and sun

so many claims are made in the name of creation,
claims of knowing and conversation

I love the humble honesty of the words:
I do not know